ANNIE FREUD

THE BEST MAN
THAT EVER WAS

PICADOR

First published 2007 by Picador
an imprint of Pan Macmillan Ltd
Pan Macmillan, 20 New Wharf Road, London N1 9RR
Basingstoke and Oxford
Associated companies throughout the world
www.panmacmillan.com

ISBN 978-0-330-44686-0

9 8 7 6 5 4 3 2 1

A CIP catalogue record for this book is available from
the British Library.

Typeset by Macmillan Design Department
Printed and bound in Great Britain by
Mackays of Chatham plc, Chatham, Kent

Visit **www.panmacmillan.com** to read more about all our books
and to buy them. You will also find features, author interviews and
news of any author events, and you can sign up for e-newsletters
so that you're always first to hear about our new releases.

For May and Dave

Acknowledgements are due to the editors of the following publications in which some of these poems first appeared: *Future Welcome* (DC Books, 2005), *Gobby Deegan's Riposte* (The Group in association with Donut Press), *Limelight, Magma, Poems for a Better Future* (Oxfam 2004), *A Voids Officer Achieves the Tree Pose* (Donut Press 2006), *Life Lines* (Oxfam 2006), *Tatler* and *Rising*.

I would like to thank John Stammers for his advice and encouragement.

On A Tame Partridge

No longer, poor partridge migrated from the rocks,
does thy woven house hold thee within its thin withies,
nor under the sparkle of fresh faced Dawn dost thou ruffle up
the edges of thy basking wings; the cat bit off thy head,
but the rest of thee I snatched away, and she did not fill
her greedy jaw; and now may the earth cover thee not lightly
but heavily, lest she drag out thy remains.

AGATHIAS, 6th CENTURY AD

Contents

1973

The women wore their scarves
so tightly wound around their necks
you'd think the occupation had returned;
their calves in putty-coloured hose
trod the pavements of the town,
strewn with dry, mysterious turds.
An advert in the paper brought us
to a door studded with nails.
There was no bell to ring, just a dot
inside a circle, and this phrase:
la sonnerie du pauvre imaginatif.

We found the 2CV just where we left it
slumped in some moribund faubourg,
whose corners never seemed to reach a turn,
and where old men raised hats in salutation
to the statue of an old buffoon.
We went to the cinema twice a day.
We cooked our omelettes in the boot.
We laughed until the money disappeared
and military service got you by the heels.
One year later, there we were again, together,
convalescent on a summer's evening,
snail-gathering at the edges of the fields.

The Things We Do

There are many things I ought to do
and I'd do them if it wasn't for *Le Pevroque*,
the tiny cinema where stark tales of sex and death
beguiled me on so many rainy afternoons
on the velvet pointillism of the screen.
I have tried to have a system, and I do have one or two;
on the cover of this notebook, I have written
Only Poetry. I have stamps. I have a plan
for a display of streptocarpus on your window sill.
Each day their graceful sufficiency will underline
the things we do, the catalogue of our intentions.

I Was the Manager of the Nipple Erectors
for Sophie and Stan

He set up home in a sunlit flat
with the daughter of a diplomat from Cairo.
They sanded the floor, lived on plain food,
bought ornaments in coloured glass,
read the Bunty in bed on Saturdays
and had long arguments about
the best way to do everything.

Alcohol was always my drug of choice
but I never got impotent.
I talked better. I danced better.
I pissed the bed, twice.

To a Coat-Stand

What Ho, my old retainer! Are we OK, you and I? No, not the OK-enquiry of will there be enough of everything to go round, or will it run out; nor the OK-enquiry of is this a party that people will remember as a real party or is someone conducting an experiment in *Normalizing Emotional Contagion Through Social Containment*. No, it's the OK-enquiry to which the only answer to be hoped for is that I will be absorbed into your wilderness of cloth.

No one will presume to ask why I, their hostess, am hesitating in the hall, with my pyramid of guacamole. Look at the room now and its lingering groups held by some strange consanguine glue so no one has to feel for long the strictures of their idiosyncrasy. And indeed, when they reclaim their coats and scarves from you, stagger down the stairs and hear their footsteps clang, will they feel somehow fulfilled, loved in spite of everything that's harsh, in spite of the exposure?

Ah, Coat-Stand! Now that your antlers are bare except for the after-image of a herringbone that haunts me marginally as I throw out the butts, tell me: where is it that we pitch our thresholds? Are there discernible stages to a person's life? My vol-au-vents puffed well, the cake cut cleanly through the fudge. But that was hours ago, when things were mixed according to their laws.

A Scotch Egg

After forty years spent in the novitiate of the abstract,
his predilection now was all for hands-on and bric-a-brac.
Hanging out, he said, was one of life's pleasures.
He loved the sense of entering the realm of the inanimate:
to riffle the flyleaves of old books made him think
of being nobbled for fivers by a wayward nephew,
and to see one's passing self in the blade of a fish-slice
was like hearing a familiar voice say *Ah, there you are at last.*
He could not forego the acquisition of a tiny cannonball,
nor the Pop-Up Book of Great Women in History,
nor a set of ocarinas painted with blue polka-dots.
These things would find their place inside the flat
beside the family of Confucian china rabbits,
a bedspread stitched by soldiers wounded in the Boer War
and, carved in balsa, a bas-relief of trysting lovers on a stile.
When Amanda praised him for the pleasure that he gave her,
that set him thinking of a scotch egg he'd bought from a stall –
delicious, the best he'd ever had: he'd remember it forever.

It's Not That You Can't Have Beautiful Things
or Have Dreams

Rather, should this waterfall be shown to you by the guide,
you'd stand there deafened by its thunder, and mute
while the voices in your mind duelled with the spirit of the place
as they always do when visiting a shrine. And from a wooden
                                          shack,
for reasons that you would not comprehend, three people would
                                          emerge
and wave at you; and you'd wonder how they ever hear each
                                          other speak
and what it means to live for ever in this place.

And when you'd turn away – as turn you must, for this stop was
                                          made
for you and the others in the minibus are waiting, and the guide
must balance all our needs – the moment closes like a door.

For I am, like you, suspicious of love and its demesne
and its mutual toast, buying books about birds, making a mental
                                          note
to call the podiatrist, and sort the chaos on the bedside table –
while consigned to writing poems about contentment, about us;
the way I am stirred now even by dry brambles on a muddy path,
his hand holding mine, wondering what he'd say if he knew
                                          what I am like.

To Have Longer Periods of Light
One has to Go North

Always water from the bottom
says the care leaflet of the patio rose.
He remembers the sense of affront he felt
when he saw *bastard* on the bathroom mirror,

and later that day, the head of a match had flown
off and burnt him when he'd struck it;
the pain had nearly made him crash the car.
He'd have to take stock.

All this is in the past, for now he's intent
on kissing another woman's abdomen.
The fish in the pond are coming up to watch
and the colours are richer than he's seen before.
Smoke billows from a neighbour's bonfire.
He notices that once again he's drunk too much.

A Voids Officer Achieves the Tree Pose

At times it seems that what she really
ought to be doing with her life
is for the ether to decide;
she'll make a film about an early time
before thought or cloth or pity or desire,
when all was flabby, all obscure, half-baked,
until the moment when a silk-worm sank its jaws
into the fibres of a mulberry leaf.

As a delaying tactic, she bangs another Frenchman.
They meet in a bar so crowded that, after shouting
for half an hour at one another, they take a taxi
to his place. She has had to repress her dismay
at his jacket, and when at last it's off and she touches him,
she recalls the final parting with her therapist;
someone who'd wear that shade of lipstick
must lack the judgement to unmask her ruse.

This is a life lived in a lunch break
when your desires have been pushed away
and the corporation's discourse is about as interesting
to you as the microbiology of the ant.
That's when some new word or thought
suggests a whole new set of possibilities;
and standing on one leg, in prayer, she knows
her real deficiencies have yet to flower.

The Inventor of the Individual Fruit Pie
for Jo

The sort of thing he thought made life worth living
was the knowledge that Mae West was real, that she lived,
and that she made the Big Time. He wondered whether
Schopenhauer would have got the point of her or not.
Then he said, *'Here is a man; he's on his own;*
there's something in the air about to expand, something out there . . .
he's smoking a cigarette, but I could replace it
with a pie that catches the mood of the moment,
and I will meet that mood,
that opportunity for careless satisfaction.
And on the other side of town,
a girl in a white dress walks along,
brushing the fence with the tips of her fingers;
she could be eating the very same pie.
And my pies will grow and multiply.
Apple, Blackcurrant, Peach and Gooseberry will be mine.
I visualise pleasures that do not pin you down,
a nation of consumers of my soft-cornered square
hand-held to their open mouths on cliff-tops and village greens,
in pavilions and on promenades, at steering wheels on the Great
                                                    West Road,
and at home on tables laid for four with plates and spoons and cream
and I will make the Big Time.'

Like What You Get When You Play It Backwards

I knew a man who had a way with women.
He'd come in and sit down at a table and talk
them into bed. And when you considered the others,
the regulars - with their constructs about life,
their Gauloises, their lingo, their Zippo lighters,
their aviator jackets with *The Glass Bead Game* protruding –
it made a lot of sense. He hardly ever had any
cigarettes. And always said 'May I have a cigarette?'
Then he would describe a prototype machine of his
for listening to music while walking down the street
or he'd make a drawing on the inner lip of a fag packet
of the scapula of a long-extinct amphibian horse,
or the configuration of classical London squares,
or a most wonderful fish soup someone called Monique
had made for him. But he never gave away too much –
no sectioning orders, no feuds with estranged wives,
and nothing that would set you on a pedestal.
Sometimes he'd open a piece of paper on which
there were long lists of words: I remember 'sackbut',
and also 'vestibule'. This was before films began
to be made about people like him so you weren't thinking
"Hey, where've I heard that before?" Yes, there was
something Buster Keatonesque in the clarity of his iris
and in his nude appeal. Once I saw a girl playing
with the red wax pooling down from the candle
in the bottle that others had been playing with
and he took her hands in his and said *Don't* and she stopped.

The Villa
for Carl

The grounds are enormous and it's strangely exclusive,
though my calls are monitored. I get to cook for myself.
The place is full of real crazies, not at all like me.
Hee hee hee, I hear you say. The staff seem more like
students at an art school, but maybe that's because
some of them wear skirts and trousers at the same time.
I heard that one of them has written a book based on
her experiences. You can't tell anything from their faces.
They seem very young to have so much responsibility
but maybe that's because I expect people to be old.
They carry these heavy bunches of keys. There's a girl
who arrived last weekend in a pink tracksuit
and has been lying face down on her bed ever since
in exactly the same position, still clutching her handbag;
she's the kid-sister of a girl in a girl-band called Bartleby.
Yesterday, I found a room with a table-tennis table in it.
A man called Mike appeared at the door and asked me to play;
we played all afternoon and I won almost every game.
There's a Chinese girl who sits at the window looking out
at the huge trees. If anyone goes near her, she turns her head
by a micro-degree so that all you can see is the line of her cheek
and a tear sliding down it. She is called Heng Li Ma.
One thing bothers me: there's no sense that anyone
is ever going to say anything about me being here.
I'm thinking of writing a film script about it.

The Best Man That Ever Was

I was never expected to sign the register
    as all was pre-arranged by his general staff,
but I did it out of choice and for the image that I made
    with the stewards and the bellboys,
my gloves laid side by side, and his Party rings that I hid
    from my family (it was torment, the life
in my family home, everyone smoking and rows
    about guns and butter at every inedible meal
and my aunts in their unhinged state, threatening suicide),
    and as I wrote my signature along the line
the letters seemed to coil like the snake
    saying, *I am here to be with Him.*

There were always little jobs to do
    in preparation for his coming – dinner to order,
consideration of the wine-list, hanging up my robe,
    a dab of perfume on my palms.
But it was never long before I found the need to pay
    attention to the corded sheaf of birch twigs
brought from home to service our love-making.
    How he loved to find it, ready for his use,
homely on a sheet of common newspaper –
    A Thing of Nature, so he said, *so fine, so pure.*
He'd turn away and smooth his thinning hair,
    lost as he was in some vision of grandeur.

And having washed and dried his hands with care
        and filled our flutes like any ordinary man,
the night's first task would come into his mind.
        He'd bark his hoarse, articulate command
and down I'd bend across the ornamented desk,
        my mouth level with the inkstand's claws,
my cheek flat against the blotter; I'd lift my skirts,
        slip down my panties and sob for him
with every blow. And I saw visions of my own: daisies,
        sometimes brown contented cows, dancers' puffy skirts,
a small boat adrift on a choppy sea; and once a lobster sang
        to me: *Happy Days Are Here Again!*

He'd tut at the marks and help me to my feet
        and we'd proceed into the dining room
and laugh and drink and raise the silver domes
        on turbot, plover and bowls of zabaglione.
You'd think he'd never seen a woman eat. Once he took
        my spoon out of my hand and asked me, *Are you happy?*
I'd serve him coffee by the fire and tend the logs.
        He'd unknot his tie. I'd comb my hair.
He'd make a phone call to no one of importance
        and we'd prepare for rest. There never was a man
so ardent in the invocation of love's terms:
        liebling, liebchen, mein liebe, mein kleine liebe!

and always the same – and in the acts: the frog, the hound,
    the duck, the goddess, the bear, the boar,
the whale, the galleon and the important artist –
    always in the order he preferred –
eyes shut and deaf to the world's abhorrence
    churning and churning in his stinking heaven.
It's over. But it is still good to arrive at a fine hotel
    and reward the major-domo's gruff punctilio
with a smile and a tip and let the bellboys slap my arse
    and remember him, the man who thrashed me,
fed me, adored me. He was the best man that ever was.
    He was my assassin of the world.

A Retreat in an Edwardian Manor House

The Welcome Session takes pace in The Barn after Tea. I am handed an oval card with a waterlily on the front and *SURRENDER!* printed on the back. The blood rushes away from my head. I will fight to the death.

Last to arrive, a man with his bedding hanging round his neck; he is *just looking forward to making a good connection with ... people,* but I am suspicious, hung as he is with so much Mexican silver. I notice a woman with coral toenails. Suddenly everyone seems to be wearing semi-precious stones.

Day One finds us emboldened by Guinevere, all plucked dome and green-gowned carnality. The call goes up for dressing table mirrors to be placed upon our altars, in accordance with the Rock of Baroque. We have paid in advance and must change our lives.

By mid-afternoon, we will have reappraised the hyperreality of these artificial fruit, especially the gleam on the grapes and the peach's fuzzy globe. Will we get hung up on a configuration of turrets? Is it the Rack of Disbelief we're on? Or is it just the sound words make that buys our compliance?

And, when one of our circle breaks down on Day Two, the long-held griefs – like maddened chessmen, each one with its reasons and lost opportunities – will make their moves and tell their stories to the world. The steam from the laundry and the chunk of the woodcutter's axe will be our moral base.

Our connectedness had grown wormy and each now goes his separate way, either in the closed circuitry of will or in vacuity of the mind, but always propped, always with a vehicle – be it an envied pencil case, a display of knowledge of the history of the holiday, or a bolt of yellow silk outside the cash-and-carry in the nearest town. The real world now clamours at the gate.

Even so, there comes a time where each one, from within the unpruned coppice of his wounded loves, will hear his fetish-queen call out his name and take a stroll with her along meandering paths to view the dusty mirror of the lake, and on to higher, and yet higher ground, where the wild garlic thrives in shimmering grass, whose uses are limited by nothing.

The Most Beautiful Bottom in the World

When I admired the photograph in your kitchen
you told me that it was of a statue of a boy

famous for having the most beautiful bottom in the world
and that the emperor who loved him

built a great library in his honour,
but the boy with the beautiful bottom died

before the library could be built
and you can't remember the emperor's name

except that he was one of the most distinguished,
if not *the* most distinguished, of all the Roman emperors.

You kissed me. I drove away.
And all that's left is what you said about the photograph,

and me going through a red light
on the Bayswater Road

and the shiny touts on Queensway
trying to get you to eat

in their Lebanese restaurants.

The Manipulation of Words

I jot one down and, like a sunbather,
it turns and looks at me as if to say,
OK, you've written me down. Fine!
Go and amuse yourself somewhere!

And here I am now on this beach,
strewn with the limbs of old loves,
the crumpled newspapers of new love,
his crossword, my striped windbreak.

I wander down the line of surf
pocketing debris that I've pocketed before,
the half-sunk shells and flattened ovoids,
the orange and blue twists of chandler's cord.

The lozenge of this brick, worn smooth,
disparages my urge to signify
and insists there's nothing to improve,
for it's a brick that's unlike any other,

as I was, when I loved another,
and everything he loved about me then . . .
even though I knew he didn't care.
With all my force, I lob it out to sea.

Our Future – Day 1

After you have buckled on your belt
and before you have put on your jacket to go out,
I'll have reminded you to collect our plane tickets,
and stop at the cleaner's for our winter coats
or at the framer's for our print of Dürer's Hare.

When you come back,
we will have ham in a cream sauce
and *pommes vapeur* and we will make
a list of our favourite country towns –
how the old combines with the new!
You will tell me a story about how,
long ago, in a concrete hotel,
you played table tennis from morning till night
for a week with a man in a hat
and we will conclude that one gets
tired of the surreal and being alone,
and that X's unreasoned dislike of hydrangeas
is stunting her capacity to flourish;
and that you can't change other people.

The Come-Back Kid

Someone to get permanently drunk with
was all I ever really wanted.

And now that I'm almost seeing him again
do I really love him like I said I did?

His in-box is 'temporarily fucked'
with trojan horses and spywares;

being one of those Mac-users, I'm immune,
and he feels truly awful about my illness.

In the bad time, there was a magic shop
in every street of which I was a denizen.

I kept seeing pairs of identical twins flaunt
their unanimity. And for the tenth time today

I wish he'd never told me about
his deck of circular playing cards,

even if I never loved him
quite the way I said I did.

The Lost Republic of Coffee

Earmuffs are for lonely girls
on cold days out with an iPod:
he watches her, down on one knee
shackling her bicycle to the railings.
Some way behind her in the queue,
he wonders whether to speak or let her be.
She takes her Americano from the kiosk,
her lips blackened by the exercise.

He suffers seeing her new sweater
and imagines the smell of her skin.
Only a month ago she straddled me,
the wanton. How she used me.
It was always her that took the initiative.
All my women do. I'm such a creep.
They profess a liking for Patti Smith.
I'm more of an Ann Peebles man, myself.

How You Tell if Someone's Crazy in the Early Stages of a Romance

You can start by standing plumb in front of a long mirror
and clean your face till it shines like a clock in a French house.
The birds will be twittering outside and you must let them,
because ambient disturbance *is* the mansion of clear thought.
Don't put on any make-up yet because, let's face it,
that's when the judgements start creeping in. And it's *his*
                                      behaviour
you are about to examine, after all, like a beer-mat turned
between the thoughtful drinker's hands. Your shoulder-blades
should drop downwards softly as if they might cross
a fathom's depth beneath the floor. Now grab your keys,
get yourself a glossy magazine and breakfast slowly on juice,
coffee and rolls. Halfway through the second cup, you'll feel
the tail-end of your peristaltic rush and you'll relive his kiss,
something he said you can't dismiss, and the sound of spanking.

A Canaletto Orange

He remembers how she pulled him down with her laugh,
lips ghoulish with wine, kingfisher glitter on her eyelids.
'Ain't Nobody Here But Us Chickens' was playing
and when she tap-danced to it, the crowd stood agog
at such velleity and he was like a man in a blizzard.
Twenty years on, the kids grown up, the marriage gone,
it's a late-lunch at *La Baracola* with the loquacious Marianne
(these days, he deploys women's names like well-bred swear-words
or types of land-mass phenomena or famous makes of cars).
Her legs are stunning, *but that's not really the point*,
he reasons in the final seconds of his self-possession.
As he drags their Gewürztraminer from its silver bucket,
there she is, framed in an alcove, lips blocked in Canaletto orange,
one heel cocked for combat. *Christ, she's keener than I thought!*
he wheezes, as she coils herself into her throne of cane.

Interlude for Xylophone, Banjo and Trumpet

He sits on a sofa, smoking a joint. The phone starts to ring.
It's for you, says his flatmate, just out of the bath.
He strays to the window and talks with his back turned.
Got a part for me? he asks as a xylophone jingles.

In the opposite flat the gas-fire is glowing
and a lady is ironing with a fag in her mouth.
I'll be there in five minutes, he says and hangs up.

He stubs out his joint on the tail of a mermaid,
perched on the rim of the rock-pool-shaped ashtray,
checks his tie and his teeth and his hair in the mirror,
winds his scarf round his neck and lets himself out.

Outside the baker's a busker is playing a hillbilly love song
on his granny's old banjo and elderly hags are shoving
their trolleys, frantic to get to the head of the queue.

He walks down the street, takes a right then a left,
past florists, dry cleaners, cake shops and chemists,
and two prancing pugs in their little plaid jackets
glare at him hard with their soulful black eyes.

Off a crowded street market, he turns up a passage
and runs up the stairs hung with portraits of actors
into an office where women and men of all races and ages
sit reading *The Stage* with their backs to the wall
while the Management juggles three calls at a time.

Without interrupting her work for a moment,
she hands him a folder marked *Gagging and Binding –
A Play for our Times* by Fielding Carstairs.

Back on the street, the sky's turning pewter
and the custom for bootleg cassettes is declining;
outside the Tube a man with burst shoes
is playing a voluntary sketch on his trumpet
like a summons for women to take off their clothes.

Decidedly hungry, he enters a restaurant,
slips into a booth, scrutinizes the menu.
The adorable waitress stands poised with her pad.
He smiles and says *I'll have the steak,
the pie and the custard and a very large cup
of your infamous brew.*

He waits in the gloom for his meal to arrive
while a dilatory sunbeam sneaks through the curtains
and he sees, to his horror, there's rice in the salt.

At the close of his meal he asks for the bill.
Was it OK? the waitress inquires.
Yes it was, he replies – *except that your chef
made the custard with water and that is a thing
that I cannot abide.*

The Maskmaker of Wanstead

O Pimp, O Clown, O Sage, O Goddess,
O my creations, what was I doing when I made you?
Hated veteran! Dull archetype! False contemporary!
I fashion and destroy you every day, for you've become
the only thing I've got that makes me feel alive. And if
I were to leave you in the bin, you'd re-coagulate as superheroes
with fan-clubs spanning continents in the merciless flogging
of interactive yogurt and themed pyjamas; I'd be poor;
you'd be rich and famous; you'd forget me and, to boot,
the world would see its dual self in your cool stare,
and, in your brute excess, the modulations of each soul.
So if – as I think you are – you're on the rise, I'm coming too
but not tonight because you're finished and I've got new
things started in the studio. You ain't seen nothing yet.

Don't Be Too Fancy

When people speak of your endearing qualities, I think
My God, you bastard. What a lot you got away with.
When we were young, I thought you were a god
when you drove us in the Mini-Moke along the Lungolago,
your shirt bellying in the wind.

I thought the striped umbrellas, the cypresses, the vibration of
                                            the engine,
the cloud of exhaust fumes, the lorries, the softpack of *Nazionali*
on the dashboard, everything that gave me pleasure in this world
was caused by your existence

and if I could be like the outlaw girl in our favourite film,
you'd come to me one night and say *My God, I've been so stupid,*
you're what I've always wanted, and here you are for the taking.

We'd have disappeared together to an old Dolomite,
or some spongy Carpathian, and spoken a private language,
lived on rabbits and come back, grown up, wiser and forgiven.

'Nobody's Perfect'

Googling the archives of the bygone smitten,
he looks for others who have loved one-footed women
to find out, in each case, how she chose to let him know,
how, in each case, the amputation was received;
and having once possessed it, if he'd found himself possessed,
and the difference that the stump made to the act.

It yields nothing but a dozen references to Pliny's *Monopodes* –
fabled for resting in the shade of their one vast foot;
he pictures them on their backs, blissful on their stony plain,
fixed in the prehistory of love's chores, no tact needed, no fine
solicitations to be phrased, no prosthetic knowledge to be gained.
How he wishes he could stop being a person just for once!

But the fact is that he's lost his flair for solitary ease.
He's changed his toothpaste to her inferior brand;
they kiss over nothing and her absent foot – the sub-plot
of his love – usurps his thoughts and stalks his dreams;
He Googles *Goddess* and finds himself consoled
by Osgood's words to Daphne at the end of *Some Like it Hot*.

'The System'
for Liane

Another coruscating cult film's showing
in the flock-lined bowels of the complex
behind the Pumpkin Dish restaurant.
It's the story of Chang, son of indentured slaves,
and his revenge on the maniac power system;
it's set in some shark-skin republic of alley-slayings,
contract rapes, fraudulent designer accessories,
effluent from canneries, insatiable maggots
and onyx malls where women lunch with forks.

He skewers the decorated mighty to their office chairs
and sees to it that whatever fetches up in the harbour
besides the lost passports and the severed hands
lands on their blotters. In every scene, there's a white horse,
an old celebrity from the advertising days,
on whose wise back the hit-man's daughter rides
each afternoon to meet her man; but the price
gets too high and she goes over to the other side
and Chang forgets to listen to his *chi*.

At the end, there's a slow (and I hear, stunningly crafted)
scene where the hero is lured down to the river
and executed between two boats. We watch him realise
– too late – what he'd got wrong. The embittered widow
of the Minister of Justice was behind the counter-plot
and as we pan away from Chang's broken body
in her private jet, the whole thing starts up again.
This much I have gathered from the reviews.
But I'd rather be with you, darling, and your brown eyes.

The Symbolic Meaning of Things
and Reasons for Not Dying

Fighting the habits of my filthy mood,
I stood at Centre Point, soaked to the skin,
when suddenly, in the street's ecstatic fugue,
I knew that it was you I had been thinking of
and with a book about Velasquez in my hands
open at *An Old Woman Cooking Eggs,*
I saw the shadow of her knife curve in her bowl
and the third egg that I will one day fry for you
ready in her hand – and just today I notice that she's blind.

I'll intimate the prospect of a small but steaming pie
on your return from some exploit on the field –
Then, like two reptiles dressed as ordinary modern folk,
we'll grind down the nutmeg of speculative thought
and with our *double entendres,* split the air.

And if I should outlive you, would I, in the full
saturation of my grief, for ever breathe verses at your photo?
Or in the tradition of my race, rip my libidinous negligee
                                        to shreds
and stock the fridge with all your favourite snacks?
And will I, when I take my final breath,
remember when you asked me to uncross my legs?

On the Street of Dripping Branches

Imagine you'd fallen asleep on the atlas of the world
and had woken, hours later, thinking of your lover
and all the hot countries you'll never go to with him,
the afternoon sleep you'll never wake from together,
the contrast of the colours in the garden,
the village women in their black clothes
watching him walk beside you with a striped bag,
and the shyness you'll feel when he comes back to you
on the beach after a long swim
and later, on the terrace, as you read about falling dictators
while the sea crashes and the geckos walk across the ceiling,
the sound of a dog barking while you made love
and the way he'd sometimes turn nasty in social situations.

The Green Vibrator

I bought a vibrator
in cucumber green.
I'd have done better
with a robot
in a morning coat.
He'd have set fire to the place
with his amiable short circuits,
turned my whites blue
and flooded the bathroom nightly.
Friends would have asked:
How goes it with The Perfect Man?
and I'd have said: *He-sends-his-love.*
And I would have loved him,
read him Byron's letters
while he peeled the potatoes
in a frilly apron. Eventually,
I'd have painted him in the nude
with my face reflected
in his silver lunch-box.

When I go out walking
on my own, I wish
that flakes of soot
would fall from the facades
of burnt-out buildings
and mingle with the tears
that pool my eyes.

Rare London Cheeses

for my father

Rarity must have been ordained to keep desire
alive, and me, as I follow after a butterfly,
looking forward to the moment when I'll recall its yellow.
And this Saturday that will stay with me for nothing more
than how the sun surprised me with its heat
and that the sea was a blue I'd never seen before.

If I mention London, it's because of Delamere,
the sadness in the backs of terraced houses,
the chimney pots in attitudes of strife,
the feathered discolorations of the render
and the way each window seems to be leading
its own, relentless, Sickertian life.

Cheese commands respect. It has ancestral status.
It is aspirational and suggests a connoisseurship
that would exasperate were it not born of greed.
Be they swathed in muslin or dipped in ashes
they will change your humour. And *London* Cheeses?
How can I ever say what anything is like?

Rare London Cheeses is the title of a book of poems
that I picked up in a dream, from the gutter of my street.
I opened it and felt the jolt of publication
as I scanned the intention and the scope of every line.
A moment later, I awoke to find it wasn't there,
nor these words, nor my name along the spine.

Le Twelve o'Clock de Hugo Williams

Two boiled eggs,
black olives,
radishes and butter curls
in a dish
of ice cubes,
a basket of bread,
and a cold beer.
Deep-fried clams with chips
and a slice of lemon,
lettuce hearts
cut in quarters
with tomatoes and capers,
and another cold beer.
Car-keys, postcards, a biro,
a red notebook
in case
nothing happens,
and a blue ticket
for the Glovemakers' Museum.
Newspapers,
sunglasses,
coffee,
one apricot-custard tart
and the lorries
full of oranges
thundering
down the coast.

Feminine Problematics

Presume exactly what you like
about this cushion's provenance;
a village landscape stitched in felt
with church and bench and wishing well
and satin tigers dozing in the chairs
distract us from the task in hand.
I'm drawing overlapping circles round
the pompadour of my taboos.
I listen to the crunch of Hula Hoops,
I notice that I've put on weight,
I take another gulp of echinacea tea
from a cabbage-leaf shaped cup.
Adaptive, mannerist, compliant,
avoiding the volumes on the shelves,
I study the jewels of my friends.
See this girl, whose silent war-cry is,
and has been, in the march of years –
I'm Pink, so resolutely Pink am I,
that no matter that I'm a total flake,
no matter that romance wrong-foots me,
and that my life has driven me to gin –
I swear that when you see me, all you'll think
is that rosebuds have gone slumming in a limousine –
and then you'll weep and laugh and slump,
throw your wineglass at the empty grate
and piss in the dirt-box of the Übermensch.
I would give up the habit
of putting things in such absolute terms
if I could leave myself behind.

My Bird

Fucking great to have done my bird
and get the heat of the sun on my neck,
no longer to hear the hooter's howl
and live in fear of the cunting screws.

Fucking great to touch a real blanket,
to stop at a boozer for a pint of Stella,
to see a hole being dug in the road
and peel a pear with a sharpened knife.

Fucking great to have done my stretch
and winch the top off a tin of sardines,
to spend the night drawing money spiders
by the light of the TV screen.

Fucking great to stand in the shower
and take a bus to the centre of town,
to hear a woman say she's sorry
when I tread on her naked toe.

Scopophilia

Double biology was my favourite:
the slim pipette, the porcelain sink,
the mooning eye inside the microscope
where starch lay split like oyster shells
and hair like furious scratches on a film.

I took fencing as an extra for a term
because I saw a torso in a padded doublet
zig-zag through a patch of sunlight
like the fleeting shadow of the mannequin
in De Chirico's somnambulist arcades.

I was taught dissection in an afternoon;
I peeled back the membranes of a rat
and pinned them like a parachute.
I saw the unresisting paws
and tiny organs neatly packed.

Nothing prepared me for this

The Ballad of Hunnington Herbert

Hunnington Herbert was her name;
she lived off Kensington Gore
in a stuccoed mansion block
owned by the late Charles Clore.

She danced in the nude for the Soft Machine;
some said she would go far.
She was often compared to Leslie Caron
with her smile and balcony bra.

Monkeys were in vogue back then;
she kept one on a chain.
It died of mange one afternoon.
She didn't try that again.

She met a man called Milton Forbes.
They went to Afghanistan.
I've a photo of her on a rock
with baby, gun and man:

lovely she looked with her silky hair
and her face turned to the sun.
Eventually she got away.
It hadn't all been fun.

The last time I saw Hunnington,
the King's Road was hot and dry.
Hail, Dark Intellect, she said,
Hail, Fair Chump, said I.

The Tragedy of the Passing Cloud Smoker

In summer he took his mother to the lakes
for her cure. They would have lunch
on the terrace: insalata tricolore,
vitello tonnato e fragole del bosco.

She'd wipe her mouth and say:
Would you mind very much if I skip coffee?
The masseuse has pummelled me half to death
and I must keep up to date with my diary.

He'd take the vaporetto to the other shore
and merge with the families in the streets
or he'd drive into town to the casino
and play roulette for half an hour
or just watch the action at the table,
the mottled hands and sparkling stones.

He'd go back to the hotel with a gift for her:
a basket of marzipan sea-shells or a pair of gloves
bought from a beautiful glossy-haired assistant
in a boutique behind the basilica.

At seven she would appear on the *piano nobile*,
with her hair done, all ruffles and gauzy swags,
dithering on bow legs, brandishing a postcard.
Listen to the latest from that sister of yours –
in love, she insists, with a marvellous man!
Angelo! Ancora uno champagne cocktail per favore.
Molto freddo. My son will have a beer.

At night, there were always women on the terrace –
usually in pairs – sympathetic and good listeners,
and best of all he liked the women of the brothel
who welcomed him and understood his needs.

Under Starter's Orders

What's a filly to do if you hit her with a crop
and tug on her reins at the same time?
I was still so bedevilled by filial loyalty
that I actually thought they minded what I did.

In April of that year, four brown-clad hermits
agreed to break their silence for my sake.
They debated long and the answer eluded them.
Could these bumbling phantoms cut the mustard?

They resumed their task and at dawn, a spokesman
was able to report the following conclusion:
– *You will understand and learn to bear the separation*
when you understand the nature of the attachment.

I dressed for dinner remembering my own angry cry:
– *You expect me to study these fine discriminations*
when my heart's been broken in two?
– *Yes, exactly.*

And now that no one knows who I'm with,
I pierce the puckered dumpling on my plate
and release the greasy duck-web at its core.
My face is wet with steam.

The Next Time

Can tonight be the next time that we meet?
It might be better not to bring the car.
I'll stay just forty minutes in the pub
and find my way from there to where you are.

The summer breeze rebukes my burning face.
I feel the jolt when jumping from the bus;
at the stop, I'm almost in your loft.
The water's waiting in the taps for us.

Honey crystallizes in cold weather.
Herds of zebra inch across the plain
and skeletons tell jokes in foreign tongues
until you crush me in your arms again.

Valentine Card

Had I made a summer pudding,
had I driven through the night
and watched you lose your shirt
at the tables every night –

had I been your faithless muse
with a little touch of camp,
held my lamp up to your mirror
held my mirror to your lamp –

had I listened to your mother
when she warned me of your faults,
I'd have questioned my commitment,
I'd have had some second thoughts.

And now we are together
and vow we'll never part:
the squirrel's got my fat-ball
and you have got my heart.

The Death of a Bat

Your text-message reads *bat dead*
and I see its feeble pulse give out,
bash itself twice against the bulb
after one last flight around the room.

I see you pick it up and murmur
words of comfort in its ear
to mark the end, and ease
its passage through the Bardos.

Here's man. Here's woman.
Here's life and love and death,
the consequence of playing it by ear,
the vacancy when tenderness has fled.

I see you later in the week and ask you
if you buried it. *What?* you say. *The bat,* I say.
It was my battery, you snap.
You take everything so seriously.

Sausages and Flowers

Don't practise your cauterising tactics on me, for I am as sentient
as your sick-note is transparent and my protest will bleed
                                        your portfolio
of its hues, blight your caseload and dismantle your druidical
                                        theories.

The cupping gesture of my hand around your balls will not
                                        submit
to your interpretation; it is the last transaction of our passion's
                                        slump.
I already knew I'd lost you and was becoming your opponent.

You call me *Madam*, yourself, the *One True Son of the Subjugated
                                        Masses*,
the self-appointed wielder of the instruments of casual spite.
You, who wooed me once with sausages and flowers.

Far better to turn away from me than repeat the accusations
spoken by many a better man than you. They didn't work then.
They never will. You've forced me to reassess my stock of
                                        weapons.

Get yourself acquainted with that whimpering fanatic
and the unbelievable softness of your skin. I'm giving up,
because I've got to – worrying about the state you're in.

The Last Kiss

Wind down the window, she mimed at him
and she kissed him one last time.
Her tongue already tasted of other men.

Here darkness fell suddenly every day;
the young men tipped their girlfriends
off their laps and they would walk to the edge
of the village on the unmade road.

With his arm around her shoulders,
she crocheted white rosettes while she walked,
keeping the dogs off them with a kick,
calling out to the other girls and laughing
in her own harsh language.

In the town there was a street of shops
that sold nothing but ornate knives, another,
lined with tiny booths where clubbing dresses
hung from the ceiling. If you wanted one,
the shopkeeper got it down for you with a hook.
By nightfall, he'd be in Trieste.

The Untameability of Subject Matter

Every time I buy a chair
something happens.
I'm just about to pay the man
and there I see a spectral word
etched in the steamed-up window
of the Vietnamese across the road
and I am drawn by gem-like sweets
in guava-scented mini-marts
where you can buy gold foil for soup
and every chocolate bar is out of date.

I'm scrabbling in my bag for cash
and see it, glowing like a splash
of fresh-spilt blood,
in a shop across the road
from Basing House Yard.

Nothing spectacular has happened.
It's as ordinary as the memory
of the way each time you drew back into yourself
in the hour before you left.

This is a fuck of a chair.

The Study of Disease

He knew her immediately for who she was;
and she, though aghast at his raincoat
and the almost sacerdotal manner of his greeting,
led him up Copenhagen Street
in blazing sunlight
and spoke of a recent dream she'd had
of pale blue missiles arcing in the sky
while her heart thudded like
a boot against her ribs.

In a bar they exchanged jokes, one each.
He talked about his work, the study of disease;
that pleased her, and she felt a shadow at last
get up and leave her to her own devices.

The badger snarling in the taxidermist's window,
the women at the bus stop with their shopping,
and the bus itself – all seemed suddenly benign.

She sat on his hand throughout the journey.
The conductress did not come to take their fares –
something he remarked on later
when he spread her out in several different ways.
In the lull they talked, drank wine, and ate quails' eggs.
He watched her as she cracked hers on the wall above the bed.

To a Window on the Caledonian Road

I look at you and then I look away
as if you were a disfigured face;
perhaps the rooms have been partitioned.
Your curtain is bridal but unhemmed.

Behind you, a woman lights a cigarette
and throws her lighter at the tiger on the bed.
She is sitting at a dressing table
piped with gold, snipping the silk bows
from her shoes before taking out her baby
in his stroller to have his ears pierced,
and to have silver comets painted on her nails.

No one monitors you, for you are on the road
that only changes to become more like itself.
I like you because you're positioned oddly,
and because you remind me of a time
when houses went unpainted
and because you have nothing
to do with my depression.

The Truth of the Matter About All Your *Things*

You talk about people who treat you badly
with many de*tails*. They may criti*cise* you,
or com*pete* with you, or you com*pete* with them.
You feel they are giving you a very hard *time*.

They may sometimes treat you quite well,
or not *so* bad, or badly as you have said.
They are not you, these other people.
They have many things: you *like* them.

These things you like belong to them. *Not to you*.
You have *your* things. They are yours.
You might like these things a lot, or *love* them.
They are all you have. Only your things are yours.

Declan

I will look after Declan, you know that.
It's probably going to be awkward at first,
because of his mother going off so suddenly.
And there's no way of knowing whether
or how often she'll call him or even whether
she'll send him presents on his birthday.
Luckily, because he's still quite little,
we'll be able to talk about her without it
seeming like some kind of a performance,
but what will it be like when he's older?
I suppose there's no point thinking so far
ahead, when we don't even know where
he's going to be sleeping tonight. I mean
all of his things, clothes, toys, homework –
his familiar stuff scattered all over London
in different people's houses, but actually
I imagine that side of things is going to be
less of a problem to sort out. It's the legal aspect
that makes me quail. I wish to God I hadn't
said I'd work today, but there's a stack
of end-of-term papers to mark and it's not
something you can just drop on someone else.
Well, whatever, it'll all get done somehow
by someone. Don't get up just yet. Hold me.

Which Ever Way You Twiddle the Knobs

Some things won't lie down or even stay. After a night
of repetitive thumps from the flat upstairs, a blind
flips up, making the acorn swing. One casement leads
into another; a cup of tea, knocked over by a fox's brush,
floods the estuary, where a ship slides from a tape recorder,
disguised as a radio, and whichever way you twiddle
the knobs, your story's completely erased –
not one single word remains – and out of the mouth
of *Maria*, kneeling by your bed like a discarded sister,
it's disgorged on ticker-tape and you know it's corrupted.

When the toaster's smoking like a bombed monument,
the letters fall on the mat and the cat says *why*,
out of the bony head of the absorbed child
a green shoot breaks. Feeling a little strange,
she rushes to the mirror, and watches it swell;
parting the leaves, she sees rising from her crown,
a bud unfolding like a dancer's underskirts,
crackling gold, unfurling with glory. And you
went on thinking it was just a matter of *suddenly* –
say but the word and the world would change.

Some things won't lie down or even stay.
Autumn colour bores them and they know you'll try
to catch their mood, and get them to let you whisper a tale
of a night in the reeds in a flat-bottomed boat,
of avenues of shadows and the gas-man's mistake.
These I have ransacked, snapping up clues
where they lay. And some things won't stand still
or even stay, like the reptile who took his leave
as soon as the river dried and scuttled away as the blind
flipped up, never to return to you, unless disguised.

The Unthinkable

If I had a rocking-horse
it would be rocking.

The blankets would have stiffened
through disuse.

The characters in the novels
on my shelves
wouldn't even bother
to work out their destinies:

they'd sit and watch the rain
on the window,
as I am doing.

The Small Book of Tropical Miracles

I thread my needle. The TV is on. I sigh for Lee Van Cleef.
I worship Katy Jurado. The model for my embroidery is Das
Kleine Buch der Tropenwunder. I exult in the three-dimensional
until each pistil quivers in its follicle and lacewings flit among
the coral trumpets under the lidless gaze of the axolotl.

When I started this commission, did I foresee I'd be as lost as
a seventeenth century sorbetier, crushing loquats in sugar for
the Infanta while his lump of ice, ordered from the Baltic, lay
melting on the lepers' road? That the order for his execution had
already been signed, and that four hundred years hence, he'd be
the model for the protagonist of a twelve million Dollar flop?

This is what I think about, sewing flowers on second-hand
clothes, under the illuminated magnifier. I switch the channel
to the Snooker Championships and as my hero bends to pot
the pink, I get closer and closer to what I really mean.

Preferring Goats

The artists sit talking about their sexual preferences.
One likes tennis players and their thick elastic drawers,
another only likes girls that other men like.
Drawing a curve in the air with his finger,
Picasso says he prefers them *comme ça;*
Francis Picabia says he likes girls who don't want to be with
                                              him very much
but not professionals because they really don't want to be
                                              with him at all.

Giacometti's brother says:
Moi, je préfère la chèvre.

To Get a Lettuce

Orange lights rotate on top of cars
parked at angles on the grass.
Six people in their party clothes
are led away for questioning.

Like someone stepping out
to get a lettuce for today's lunch,
I take the long way round the house,
past the collapsed greenhouse

and brimming water butt.
A two-way radio crackles.
If I am seen it will be clear
that I have done nothing.

Pankow Park – Berlin

for Antje and Kai

The loose-socked mothers, hip with nerves,
layer-dressed, like multiple inner selves,
unstrap their offspring from complex carts.

All is heroic, even the leaves, the plunging hooves
and the cranes; Siegfried lopes along the Unter den Linden,
talking to Sybilla, Ute and Amelie on his hands-free.

A man with documents and pipe sings as he walks.
From the bridge a toddler breaks the calm:
Eine tote schlanger! Eine tote schlanger!

The Small Mammal House

I dream of an encounter in a bar.
He asks: *What's the part of sex you like least?*
Good question, mutters the God of Slime
that sits astride my liver. And I say:
It's the moment when I know for sure
that it will happen with this person.
It's like looking down on a logging operation;
the cutters advance through the trees
and you know . . . that'll be the next one to fall.

I did not keep my powder dry
and that is why I left my heart
in the Small Mammal House,
bulging like a drawstring purse,
eating fruit salad in the darkness.

White

I remember Bob Peck in *Edge of Darkness*:
a girl was murdered and her white vibrator
was found by her father in her bedside table.
He kissed it; he was a Detective Inspector.

You don't expect a Detective Inspector
to tenderly kiss a white vibrator,
especially one that belonged to his daughter,
especially one that was literally murdered.

It's years ago and I still remember
the shock of his grief, the loss of his daughter,
the tender kiss on the white vibrator,
the Inspector kissing the white vibrator.